ZANY, BRAINY ANIMALS

HOW ANIMALS COMMUNICATE

DR. ASHLEY WARD AND ANDY ROWLAND

PowerKiDS press

Published in 2026
by The Rosen Publishing Group, Inc.
2544 Clinton Street, Buffalo, NY 14224

First published in Great Britain in 2024 by Wayland

Editors: Elise Short, Jenni Lazell
Designer: Rachel Lawston

Cataloging-in-Publication Data

Names: Ward, Ashley, author. | Rowland, Andy, 1962-, illustrator.
Title: How animals communicate / by Dr. Ashley Ward, illustrated by Andy Rowland.
Description: Buffalo, NY : PowerKids Press, 2026. | Series: Zany, brainy animals | Includes glossary and index.
Identifiers: ISBN 9781499454123 (pbk.) | ISBN 9781499454130 (library bound) | ISBN 9781499454147 (ebook)
Subjects: LCSH: Animal communication--Juvenile literature.
Classification: LCC QL776.W373 2026 | DDC 591.59--dc23

Manufactured in the United States of America
CPSIA Compliance Information: Batch #CSPK26. For further information contact Rosen Publishing at 1-800-237-9932.

Picture credits:
Shutterstock: aDam Wildlife 29c; Sergius Beicher 9t; Bejim 19; Willyam Bradberry 8; Gan Chaonan 27t; Alex Cooper Photography 21l; Henner Damke 7t; Costas Anton Dumitrescu 27b; Fidel 18; Jayden Gunn 22r; Hendradive 20; Eric Isselee 4c,16t; A Jansco 6; Anan Kaewkhammul 7b; Anita Kainrath 9b; Ron Kolet 22cr; David A Litman 21; Doug McLean 11; Sayan Moongklang 10; Soumyajit Nandy 16b; ND700 14bl; Noicherrybeans 4t; Alexander Potapov 5tc, 5tr; Lauren Proctor 23; Nataly Reinch 28r; Serg64 13t; Vladimir Strnad 24; Mark Sully 25t, 25b; Mr Payu Upathum 14br; Imogen Warren 22c; Xaki646 26t; Yui Yuize 12; zstock front cover c.

CONTENTS

HOW DO ANIMALS COMMUNICATE?

Chances are that when you think about communication, the first things you think of are words. You might imagine chatting with your friends face-to-face or maybe messaging them. It's different for other animals. They don't have language like we do, but all animals need to get their message across.

So how do they do it? Some use **SOUNDS**, like us. Others use **SMELLS**, or **VISUAL DISPLAYS**, or even **TOUCH**. Many of them use a mix of all of these things. We might not realize it, but animals communicate with each other all the time!

Wouldn't it be **AMAZING** to understand what animals are saying? The good news is that all it takes to communicate with animals is to understand a little of their language, to appreciate how they say things, and why.

TALES FROM THE LAB

Understanding animal behavior is not an easy task. First, scientists watch animals living their life.

That's how they get their ideas. Then they test these ideas by running experiments. If they're lucky, they'll find out something that no one has ever known about animals, which is the most exciting thing possible! In this book, you'll find many amazing discoveries about how animals communicate.

CHIMP CHAT

Chimps are our closest relatives and we have plenty in common with them. However, the way that they chat is quite different to the way that we do. Unlike us, chimps do a lot of their talking by all kinds of imaginative gestures!

What do we mean by a gesture? Think about when someone asks if you'd like some boiled Brussels sprouts. Maybe you shake your head–that's a gesture, as is a shrug or a thumbs up to say, "Yes, please." Although gestures take a back seat to talking when we're communicating, chimps rely on these signals when they're interacting, and they have **MORE THAN 60** different gestures!

They tear tiny bites from leaves to tell another chimp that they like them, rub parts of their body to show others that they want to be groomed, or hold out a leg to their offspring, which means "Climb on my back." There's a lot going on in chimp conversations, but you have to watch as well as listen!

TALES FROM THE LAB

Back in the 1970s, scientists were interested to see if chimps could learn to speak human languages. The way that they did this was to teach chimps sign language–the kind that's used by people who are hearing impaired. It was an AMAZING success. One chimp, called Washoe, learned 350 different words and could chat with her handlers!

DOLPHIN DECLARATIONS

When you want to get a friend's attention in the playground, you probably just shout their name. Until recently, we thought humans were the only animals that did this, but that was until we started studying dolphins. It turns out that each dolphin has its own, unique call, known as a **SIGNATURE WHISTLE** that it uses, just like a name, to identify itself.

Unlike us, dolphins aren't given their own name by their parents. Instead, they choose their own when they're young. They do this by listening out for the signature whistles of other dolphins and choosing bits from each one to invent their own unique whistle.

Dolphins learn their friends' signature whistles and use these to greet them when they meet. When a dolphin hears another call out its signature whistle, it replies with the same call as if to say: **"I'm here!"**

As well as signature whistles, scientists have identified lots of other sounds that dolphins make. They squeal with delight when they accomplish a task, they **BUZZ** at each other when they're angry, and they **SQUAWK**, **SCREAM**, and **BRAY** too. We just don't know yet what all of these sounds mean ...

ANT ROADWAYS

Have you ever had the terrible experience of enjoying ice cream on a hot summer's day, only for the melting treat to drop from its cone and fall with a **SPLAT** onto the ground? If you have, maybe you've noticed that within a few minutes, ants have gathered at the scene of the disaster and are happily digging in.

How did the ants know it was there? Most ants are either blind or have very poor sight, so they didn't see it. Instead, they use the ant version of a nose! Once one of them finds it, they tell **ALL THEIR FRIENDS** about this unexpected sugary banquet on the path.

To tell each other this kind of good news, ants communicate using chemical messages called **PHEROMONES**. The first ant to discover your fallen food heads back to the nest and, as it goes, leaves an **INVISIBLE** but **SMELLY** trail behind it. When the other ants sniff the scent, they can follow the trail all the way.

The ability of ants to use pheromone trails in their communication is pretty impressive, but scientists have found that there's another way that ants make sure their nestmates find food quickly. Rather than just relying on the trail, the ant will **PICK UP** another ant and **CARRY IT** to the food. Scientists call this **TANDEM RUNNING**.

FLOWER DANCING

Just like ants, bees do a lot of their talking using pheromones. But honey bees have one of the most **AMAZING** forms of communication in the whole animal kingdom. They tell each other where flowers are by **DANCING!**

When a honey bee finds a perfect flower, it **ZOOMS** back to the hive to tell the other bees about it. To do this, it dances in a figure 8, waggling its abdomen on the way back to the center of the 8. This is why it's called a waggle dance. The other bees must pay attention to the direction the dancer moves, because this tells them where they need to fly to find the flower.

The dancer also tells the others how far they should fly—a longer dance means they have further to go. And if it buzzes excitedly while it's doing all this, the dancer is telling the other bees that this is a **FANTASTIC FLOWER!**

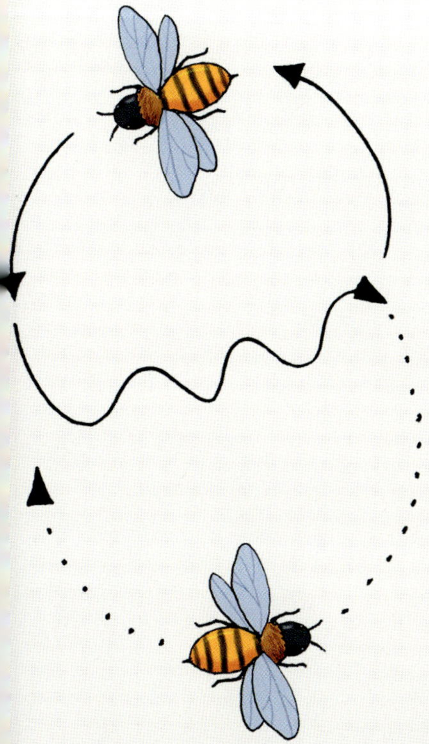

TALES FROM THE LAB

The secret communication used by bees was uncovered by a German zoologist called Karl von Frisch, who devoted his life to understanding these wonderful little insects. He announced that he'd worked out what the bees were telling each other almost a century ago, but lots of people didn't believe him. It took years before everyone agreed that he was right, and that these simple animals are able to share the location of a flower.

HOW A LOBSTER SAYS HELLO

Imagine you've just met up with one of your friends after not seeing them for a few days. How do you greet each other? You might shout "Hi!" or hug or high-five one another, but I hope you don't do what lobsters do. Because when lobsters meet, their way of saying hello is to **PEE IN EACH OTHER'S FACE!**

It might not sound very nice, but by doing this, lobsters give each other lots of information, such as who they are, how strong they are, and even what sorts of food they've been snacking on lately.

The reason they say hello in this rather strange way is that lobsters have poor eyesight and struggle to make sounds, so if they want to recognize one another, they have to use their sense of **SMELL**. Using this, they can work out whether the other lobster is a rival, a potential mate, or just their next-door neighbor.

TALES FROM THE LAB

How do we know that lobsters do this? After all, we can't usually see lobster pee. It looks just like the water that they live in. To work out what they're doing, scientists give them a harmless dye called fluorescein, which turns their urine bright green. Then when two lobsters meet, we can see their heads disappear in a great fluorescent cloud of pee.

SECRET MESSAGES

Animals communicate all the time, but much of what they're saying goes unnoticed by us. Did you know that if you tickle a rat, it actually **LAUGHS?** The rodent's giggle is **ULTRASONIC**, which means it's a sound so high-pitched that we can't hear it!

At the other end of the scale, elephants converse using deep, bass sounds. We don't hear these either. They're too low for us to pick up on.

So why do many animals use communication channels that only they can hear? Partly it's to do with their size: big creatures tend to make deep sounds, while high-pitched noises come from smaller animals. Listen to a Chihuahua and a Great Dane barking and you'll see what I mean.

But it's also partly to do with animals wanting to keep their conversations **SECRET!** Then they can avoid the attentions of eavesdroppers, such as predators, who might mean them harm.

TALES FROM THE LAB

In the 1980s and '90s, an American scientist called Katy Payne was the first to discover that elephants were using a secret communication channel. She could see that elephants would occasionally stop walking and become alert, but she didn't know why. She had the idea that maybe they were using deep sound to chat, so she used special technology to investigate. Sure enough, the equipment picked up the sounds, allowing us to listen in for the first time!

FIGHTING TALK

Have you ever woken up very early on a spring or summer's morning and heard the birds outside singing like crazy? This is what we sometimes call the **DAWN CHORUS** because lots of different birds sing most enthusiastically when the sun begins to rise.

Although the tweets and songs might sound nice to us, this is important bird business. Each bird is singing a warning to their rivals, telling them to **STAY OUT** of their territory! They're really saying, **"This is mine! MINE!"**

Why do birds go to all this effort to sing first thing in the morning? Scientists have investigated this, and it turns out that it's extremely important for each bird to let the others know it's still in control of its territory as soon as they all wake up. If they don't do this as soon as it starts to get light, other birds come to investigate if they can claim this little patch of the neighborhood for themselves!

At the same time, songbirds are hoping to attract the attention of a potential mate, by showing off how good they are at singing!

CONVERSATIONS WITH CUTTLEFISH

Cuttlefish are amazing undersea creatures, closely related to octopuses and squid. They spend a lot of their time chatting with each other.

The way that they communicate is by moving their arms in different ways and flashing incredible colors and patterns across their bodies. Their skin is capable of changing color almost instantly, and because of the way it's linked up with their brains, their skin reveals what they're thinking.

When two cuttlefish meet, they can tell each other how they're feeling with different colors and patterns for different moods. And if cuttlefish don't want anyone else to know what they're saying, they can keep their conversations private. They do this by only using the color signals on the side of their body facing the cuttlefish they're chatting with.

TALES FROM THE LAB

While diving, marine biologist, James Herbert-Read noticed that cuttlefish hold their arms in different ways whenever they are face to face with another cuttlefish.

Since cuttlefish can't speak, James reasoned that this was how they chatted with each other. So, he swam up to them and, pointing his hand toward them, held his fingers out in a variety of patterns. The cuttlefish started answering him by holding their arms out in just the same way! James had discovered how to chat to cuttlefish. The only problem is that he never knows what he's saying to them!

LYREBIRD LYRICS AND OTHER MIMICS

Birds have the most amazingly complex voices in the animal kingdom. Some of them can even be taught to say a few words, although their squawky voices might sound funny to us.

As good as some birds, such as parrots, are at imitating, there's one bird that puts every other animal in its shade. Lyrebirds live in Australia, where they copy the sounds made by at least 20 other birds and build them into their own song. The effect is that when there's a lyrebird in the forest, all the other birds get hopelessly confused.

Lyrebirds not only duplicate the songs of other birds, but they also expertly copy other noises, like car alarms, crying babies, and phones, to name a few. Their imitations are very accurate–just like the real thing–and it's a very strange experience to walk through the forest and hear all of these sounds!

Impressive though the lyrebird's antics are, animals always have a reason for doing things. In the case of lyrebirds, it's only the males who play these vocal games and researchers have discovered that there's a lot at stake for them. Females prefer males who are the best mimics!

ALBATROSS ANTICS

Some of the most important communication in any animal's world happens when they want to breed. That's never more the case than with albatrosses.

These enormous seabirds remain faithful to their partners for life—and that might be as long as 40 years! Even though each albatross spends months and months on its own flying over the open ocean, they make a point of returning to land every so often to find their partner.

An albatross reunion is an amazing thing to see and it involves a LOT of communication between the two birds. Facing each other, they touch beaks tenderly, spread their wings wide and take tiny steps, jiggling excitedly on the spot. They might carry on like this for an hour!

Each pair has their own routine, and they speak to each other through the language of dance. Perhaps it's no surprise that they seem so enthusiastic. After all, at this stage, they might not have seen each other for nearly a year!

Tender as the albatross's dance is, scientists think that one of the main reasons they do it is not only to renew their bonds but almost as a test. It's hard work to raise a chick and can take as long as a year, so both partners need to make sure that the other is strong and fully committed to raising a chick.

HYENA BULLETIN BOARDS

Animals have lots of different ways of getting the message across and lots of them use smells. Think about when dogs pee on lampposts or when cats spray trees or bushes. It tells other animals who's been there.

Most impressive in this respect are hyenas, which live throughout Africa in big groups called clans. Each clan has its own territory, or a place that they've reserved just for themselves. To make sure everyone knows, they post smelly messages at the edge of their territory using a horrid, stinky substance known as **HYENA BUTTER!**

If a hyena from a different clan comes along, it knows that it's in for trouble, because hyenas defend their homes fiercely!

Hyena butter isn't anything you'd want to spread on your toast. It comes from a special gland near the hyena's bottom, and they smear it on grass stems and other vegetation. It acts like a bulletin board, telling anyone who's interested which clan the territory belongs to, and when they were last here.

The reason that hyena butter smells a bit nasty is that it's full of different types of bacteria. Hyena researchers have learned that by living together, all the individuals in a clan end up sharing the same kinds of bacteria. That's important because it means that all the hyenas in a clan get to produce hyena butter with the same clan smell, so everyone knows who they are!

KEEP IN TOUCH!

One of the oldest types of animal communication uses the sense of touch—or more accurately, the ability to make and to feel vibrations.

Lots of creatures use vibrations to communicate, such as termites who bang their heads against the walls of their nest whenever predatory ants are approaching. The vibrations caused by the headbanging are picked up by the other termites, who can then run for cover.

The treehopper is another. This tiny, pea-sized insect eats plants. Groups of them gather on particularly tasty plants to feed, but as they do so, some of them act as lookouts for danger. If a predator such as a spider happens along, the lookout rapidly shakes its body, sending vibrations throughout the plant to all the other treehoppers, allowing them to scuttle to safety!

TALES FROM THE LAB

When rival spiders approach one another on a web, researchers found that they literally weigh each other up! They do this by feeling how much the web bends when another spider steps on it. Whichever is the heavier spider will win a dispute, and the lighter one will retreat. Scientists learned this by adding lead weights to small spiders and found that even their biggest, heftiest rivals turned and ran when they felt these upgraded spiders approaching!

GLOSSARY

Bacteria tiny living things

Behavior the way in which a person or animal acts

Fluorescent the light given off by certain creatures that is only visible under UV light

Mate one of a pair of animals that have babies together

Marine biologist a scientist who studies animal, plant, and microscopic life in oceans

Mimicry the act of copying the sounds or behavior of a particular animal

Offspring the child or young of a particular human, animal, or plant

Pheromones a scent given off by some animals to communicate

Predator an animal that hunts other animals for food

Prey an animal that is hunted or caught for food, usually by another animal

Territory the area an animal lives in that it defends against other animals

Ultrasonic a type of sound that is too high-pitched for humans to hear

FURTHER INFORMATION

Books

Animal Communication by Virginia Loh-Hagan (45th Parallel Press, 2025)

Science-ology!: Zoology by Anna Claybourne (PowerKids Press, 2026)

The Who, What, Why of Zoology: The Incredible Science of the Animal Kingdom by Jules Howard (Wide Eyed Editions, 2023)

Websites

Explore how animals use ultrasound to communicate and take the quiz:
www.bbc.co.uk/bitesize/topics/zxfrwmn/articles/zv3kxyc

Find out more about animals:
kids.nationalgeographic.com/animals

INDEX